SHADOW CHILD

SHADOW CHILD

P.F. THOMÉSE

Translated from the Dutch by Sam Garrett

BLOOMSBURY

First published in Great Britain by Bloomsbury Publishing Plc 2005
First published in Amsterdam 2003 by
Uitgeverij Contact under the title *Schaduwkind*
This paperback edition published 2006

Bloomsbury Publishing Plc, 36 Soho Square, London W1D 3QY

A CIP catalogue record for this book
is available from the British Library

Publication of this book has been made possible
with financial support from the Foundation for
the Production and Translation of Dutch Literature

ISBN 0 7475 7973 3
9780747579731

10 9 8 7 6 5 4 3 2 1

Typeset by Hewer Text Ltd, Edinburgh
Printed in Great Britain by Clays Ltd, St Ives plc

All papers used by Bloomsbury Publishing are natural,
recyclable products made from wood grown in well-managed forests.
The manufacturing processes conform to the
environmental regulations of the country of origin.

www.bloomsbury.com/pfthomese

For Makira, for ever

Je suis toujours celle que tu respires
Paul Valéry, 'La jeune Parque'

Put up a fence today. Even though we live on the city's roof, high above the Valley of the Ants, there are always faces, eyes, looks. God, I hate people. Shoo! Get! Up there in our secluded garden, in any case, I clipped away all the blossoms, pruned off all the buds. I had to do something, things can't just go on as though nothing has happened, can they? The leaves are bursting out all over, there's no stopping them. Shoots and new growth everywhere. (And in the darkest corner, furtive and untouched, the alder. A drab sapling that must once have stowed itself away in old soil. Now already as big as a child.)

Fences, partitions, shears. Others dig moats, forge locks, raise bridges. Burn cities to the ground. Yet it all comes down to the same thing. Wanting to set something aright after it's too late. Wanting to set something aright *because* it's too late. Constraining, controlling, directing: the triad of impotence.

Every day we drift further from her, every step we take is a step away from her. Living on means on and on, further and further away from her. We dig in our heels against the days, but the days roll over us. They drag us along, carry us off to places which bear a remarkable resemblance to something we once knew. And yet everything's different. Did someone go and rearrange things on us, while we were away? We keep running into things, hit snags again and again, for we have no idea where in the hell we've ended up.

Our house, the house of two strangers. Do they have a child? The silence makes it hard to tell. We grope our way around. We cast about for the smell of laundered whites in clean rooms, the breath-soft calm of the afternoon nap. Happiness is something you only mention once you can no longer find it. The cotton hush, the filtered sunlight.

Quiet it is, but the wrong quiet. From all the cupboards, all the corners, panic can suddenly jump out at you. Despair lurks everywhere. We stay on our guard, we try not to look. Not at the little outfits in the laundry basket. And definitely not at the cot either, the little red blanket with the milk stain, the cap with earflaps. No! Don't look!! It's only the sickest catastrophe, hidden especially in the little things dearest to us.

We have to learn to defend ourselves, we're far too vulnerable this way. When a baby's cap strikes fear in you, you're in trouble.

The constant feeling that something's not right, that things need sorting out around here. Who clipped away all the blossoms, damn it? The garden was just starting to flower. I know, I know (things don't turn out the way they're supposed to).

We have to watch what we do, mistakes have been

made, something has gone fundamentally wrong. And meanwhile, like a stowaway in my thoughts, the spurious assumption that we'll find a way out of this. All we have to do is get organized. Losing something simply means you don't know where you put it. So take a good look around, even in the last place you'd ever think. Especially there. And tidy up after yourself right away, otherwise you'll lose track. When things don't have a place to belong, it all comes to a shrieking halt. Before you know it, hideous sorrow will have put on the little-dress-with-the-animals, and be leaving the smallest of socks around, right where you'll find them.

MISSING WORD

A woman who lives longer than her husband is called a widow, a man without his wife a widower. A child without parents is an orphan. But what do you call the father and mother of a child who has died?

On the day the calamity was to come down on us (and unfurl before us like a lily), we had trouble understanding the portents.

At first it seemed the kind of thing you'd file away later under 'anecdotes'. For the longest time, I kept clutching at the point of the story: how we all emerged unscathed. After all, isn't that how it always ends? When something's happening to you, you never know *what*'s happening to you. You're in the dark. Fear builds up around you like a wall, you can't see over it. What lies beyond you know only from hearsay. It's built of inexperienced words: words that have no idea what they're saying. So whatever we may have feared, our thoughts clung to the happy ending. That was the territory we knew. It was all just something we had to go through. On the other side, the good old, happy-go-lucky happy ending was patiently waiting for us.

That's why we missed the signs at first. We didn't see what was different, and if we happened to see it anyway, we must not have been paying attention. How often do you run into Death without seeing him? How often are you rescued without even noticing?

It's amazing, in retrospect, how normally everything

went. The blitheness of people on the verge of disaster, the stunning normalcy with which people move towards their doom. It seems that, even then, there is no life but daily life. Rather than bracing ourselves for horrors, we wonder whether this will leave us enough time to cook something later on, or whether we'll have to go to the Chinese for a takeaway. 'Later.' Our time was still running by the clock on the living-room wall.

But meanwhile, one by one, the hospital was taking over our functions.

The hopelessness of the situation would not sink in. Hope is a hardy substance. You chop it off, and it grows back again. Something is removed, shut, destroyed, and, precisely at that same spot, hope starts growing again.

We, who were no longer allowed to take our child in our arms, adapted immediately. We learned to read lips, eyebrows, fingers. I even read backs and shoulders, I read footsteps, doors, silences. Later they brought in the equipment, more and more equipment. We learned to read that as well. We learned numbers and their relationship to respiration, pulse rate, blood pressure. We learned to ignore certain beeps, and could distinguish unerringly between the various drips and tubes. They provided us with explanations, the only ones at our disposal. We wanted to understand everything, we sought a handhold in every fact, in order to keep from falling. Into bottomless nothing.

'I think she's sleeping quietly now,' you said.
'Yes,' I said.
For as long as you could say it, it might be true.

Her birth came to us like an infatuation; everything became charged, enchanted by the miracle of her presence. The world, in which I had moved without direction for so long, suddenly had a radial centre. Too bad the high C has vanished from our speech, that towering register in which the joyful rise up in rapture, stared after in amazement by those left behind on the ground floor. 'As the lily is among thorns,' I repeat after the song in my heart, 'so is my love among the daughters. Stay me with flagons, comfort me with apples: for I am sick with love.'

She's everything that was missing, we told each other. But we didn't even know who she was, this living creature, pulled from you slipping and floundering at eight-twenty on a Friday evening.

Infatuation is a state that precedes identity. Just as a person has no need of a name for his own sake (one 'knows' who one is), so too the beloved needs no name. A name would limit her without reason, because she's simply too much for a single name. Ardour prefers to sample pet words, try out sounds that are replaced the moment they fall short. Nothing is fixed, everything is possible. Each time you haven't looked for a while, she seems different. A person in love has so much to remember at once, it never works out. Looking again and again, touching again. Reading the face like a blind man, with your fingertips. Afraid to miss anything at all, to skip something, forget a thing.

The first night, with her in between us. Full-moon light through the attic window, the pillows, the sheets, the wallpaper, everything silver and blue. Just like then, the first night you stayed with me and I was unable to fathom my luck. Full moon then too: magic light, old as time, that's saved many a lost ship at sea. And now we're lying here with this amazing bundle between us. We had tidied up around the house beforehand, cleaned and rearranged it. Bought things. One must be prepared for the arrival of the beloved. But now that she's lying here in her first moonlight, her first bed, her first world, nothing else matters. All the carefully constructed explanations collapse at a breath, like paper towers of Babel on an overworked desk. The last word will always be a first word.

Does love disappear when the person disappears?
Where does the love go when the body is burned to
ashes? It flees into similes. The body has been taken
from the earth, but not all the things that remind you
of it.

'. . . thine eyes are like the ponds in Heshbon, by
the gate of Bathrabbim: thy nose is as the tower of
Lebanon which looketh toward Damascus. Thine head
upon thee is like Carmel . . .' Like, indeed, like, like.
Love looks for an embodiment it can no longer find.

The way visiting family members dissect new off-
spring in search of resemblances, I try to reconstruct
her demolished future on the basis of girlish things I
come across, along my way.

Today, too, on the street I saw forms she could have
taken. There are enough things that would fit her.
Gestures, faces, figures. That's not the problem. I saw
a little girl on the back of a bike, soundlessly grimacing
all her secrets to her mother's back; two girlfriends of
thirteen, a fat one and a pretty one, smoking filter
cigarettes in a doorway and screeching with laughter,
and, in the tram, a dark-haired princess of sixteen or
seventeen, a book open on her lap, staring pensively
out of the window. Instances in which she was poten-
tially present.

A man can love different women, all a mother's children are equally precious to her. So why can't she, who is ash herself, be entrusted to bodies which have, only in the strictest sense, never been hers?

It's hard to know the moment when I first realized she was hopelessly lost. Or rather: the moment when I finally dared to admit knowing it. For there are certain kinds of insights that first travel along with your thinking like a stowaway, silently, staying inconspicuous, a dark figure hidden away in one of the lifeboats on the top deck. You know it, with all the sneaking suspicion at your disposal you know it, it's just that you don't want to know it for sure, not yet, like with a letter you're still dreading to open. And you don't want to know it for each other's sake either, you don't want to do that to each other.

And there is something else as well. That's the matter of language, the matter of communicability. You know it, but not how to go about saying it. The tongue gropes across the palate in vain. All the words you find seem borrowed, not applicable. What's going on is not 'something like'. There are no precedents to follow.

Meanwhile the thoughts simply go on polishing away at the anecdote she'll hear later: how Mum and Dad sat up all night by her hospital bed.

Our little girl never let on. She had taken cover deep inside herself, searching in her body for something to hold on to.

Visiting hours were long over, we were the only parents left amid the sleeping children. Night crept into the ward, muffled the sounds, put out the lights. Unwatched monitors dutifully produced rows of digits, the way a sinking ship produces bubbles.

I stand, at the big window. A figure staring out. No moon in the sky, only the neon of the streetlights and lighted office buildings. The clouds are lit only from below. Behind that, darkness unto the end of time. Behind me, I know you are bending over her again, rearranging her nappy, moving aside a tube, a cable, a wire that's coming out of her or one she has to have in her, you brush an invisible hair from her face. I lean my forehead against the cool pane. Far below, traffic crawls like blood running through the city, the paved roads and streets a network of arteries, veins and capillaries, to supply even the furthest extremities of this city with living people.

So this is it, came the thought inside me. This is the worst that could happen to me, and now it's happening. Our baby is dying there, behind my back. Before long she'll be gone for ever. I knew it, but I didn't feel it. I didn't feel anything at all any more.

A stone was what I had become, all I could do was break.

Our life has fallen shut like a book we'd been reading
in bed. Now that we've picked it up again, we can't
find the page we were on. We try reading on a little,
but no, none of it seems even slightly familiar, it's like
one of those Russian novels where everyone's name
keeps changing all the time. The twists of plot don't
say a thing to us, we couldn't have been this far yet.
But even when we leaf back we never reach a point
where we can say: ah yes, I remember this part.

Maybe we've picked up the wrong book, maybe
what we have to do first is figure out what we were
actually reading.

Or are we reading this book of ours through different eyes, and does the whole story simply seem far-
fetched to us now?

You were sitting in a twin-engine plane over Texel, watching the skydivers. (I'd stayed behind, because of my fear of flying.) You were struck by how green and mountainous the island was down there. Suddenly a huge passenger plane loomed up beneath yours, a dark blue airbus, from an airline you'd never heard of. The big plane was clearly flying off course. It banked to avoid hitting you and lost its balance, one wing actually touched the water of an inland sea before it slammed into a mountainside (a dune?).

You were horrified, you'd never witnessed anything so horrendous. You were afraid it was your plane that had been at fault, that you had flown into the path of the big aircraft. But the pilot said that was impossible, passenger planes like that had absolutely no permission to fly here.

At the press conference they pretended it was no big deal after all. Everyone started acting very cool, very la-di-da. Whenever news would come in, the curtains would be drawn right away. The conference was being held in an old villa with antiques all over the place, those kinds of handed-down family heirlooms. There were lots of snooty ladies walking around who acted as though they knew exactly what had taken place (even though they hadn't been in the plane).

That made you so angry. You started shouting and stamping your feet. What gave them the right to be informed, and not you? Weren't you the one who had seen the whole thing happen right in front of your eyes? At the top of your voice, you told those stupid cows exactly what was what. After all, it was *you* who had been the eyewitness, and not them. Getting angry like that made you feel better. You were finally able to say it out loud. You became so worked up that it woke you.

I was in the living room, talking on the phone to someone from the literature council, when I looked out of the window and saw a glider trying to land in our roof garden. It was suspended in midair, as it were, it had pulled up right alongside the fence, I could look the pilot in the eye. He looked back, brash and self-confident.

The person on the other end was trying to put me through to the person I really needed, which didn't seem to be working. But since I had her, the wrong person, on the line anyway, I told her how strange it seemed that a glider should try to land in my rooftop garden, completely unannounced.

'It can't be more than five by five,' I shouted like a radio announcer. 'And,' I added in amazement, 'he hasn't damaged a single leaf.'

By this time the pilot was sitting at our dining-room

table and I had to find a chair for myself. I was struck by what an anachronism he seemed, with his World War I cavalry uniform, the goggles on his forehead and that leather cap with earflaps. The young man himself, though, looked perky and modern; I didn't completely trust him not to ply you with his charms.

I didn't want you to know I was jealous, so I pretended that the presence of this uninvited guest didn't bother me in the slightest.

Right then it occurred to me that the woman from the literature council was still on the phone, and I got up from the table. I tried to explain in an ironic tone to this woman (whom I must have known, but whose name I simply couldn't remember) how confusing the situation had become on the home front, but at the other end I heard only the canned silence of an abandoned receiver, lying on an unmanned desk.

I didn't want the pilot to see that I'd been given the brush-off, so I pretended casually to lay the phone back on the cradle. The mistake I made in doing so was that I had not spoken a single word of farewell, so he saw right through me.

The truth as unhidden thing, as Heidegger puts it, as that which one sees 'all at once', even though it was there all along. It was *you* who kept missing it. Eyes shut to the 'Unhiddenness'. The way you're unable to find a pair of scissors (even though your gaze has already passed over them a few times) on a messy counter, because you're searching in the wrong context.

The contexts or presumed connections between things often keep you from seeing the things themselves. You recognize them only in a given setting. The same way you can't place a face you see on the street, even though you're sure you've seen it before. What you lack is the proper constellation, the office where that particular face is a fixture, the counter, the ticket window, the café.

So, too, with dying. Hidden away in familiar constellations, tucked away in comforting contexts, it usually lies there resting in peace. You only see it where you ought to see it: in cemeteries, in obituaries and in poems that rhyme 'the way of all flesh' and 'we're caught in the mesh'.

But suddenly the hidden thing appears. Throws off its cover. Is dis-covered. Now that the pith is no longer covered, you can't believe you didn't see it before.

Suddenly the truth is everywhere, at the butcher's and the baker's, in the park; even in the eyes of others you see the dying go on.

Dying, it seems, cares as little for end rhymes and cemeteries as it does for other words or other places. When it comes right down to it, none of that says a thing. No form that can become meaningless enough. During dying, distinctions are not drawn but erased. No more differences, only un-difference.

Everything I've learned becomes null and void at a single blow. Experience expires. All that I have considered important no longer counts. My feelings, kept at room temperature, can't stand the chill. My hands, my arms, are too full of holes to embrace what is being lost. The only words left start with un- and in-, words that try to get away, that try *not* to say something.

I'm reminded of the Jewish survivor Paul Antschel, who, after his return from the extermination industry, turned his surname around and become Paul Celan, because he had first gone from life towards death, but was now trying to find his way from death back to life. Coming from the other direction, however, nothing looked like it was supposed to. Language, everything had been hollowed out by events. No word had kept its meaning. Everything he knew had to be disacknowledged. The words had to be taken piece by piece, syllable by syllable, and securely refitted into the silence.

Her place must still be found, he says to me. He says: 'Where she never was, there she will always remain.'

Above all, though, we miss the world we can't get to without her: that lost infinitude where everything still has its divine nature, and nothing has taken on fixed form. We needed her in order to get there. We needed her in order to believe it, to believe that life has only a beginning: windows, doors swing open, you tumble into sunlight, around you a street pops up with cars that begin to drive, everywhere you walk by flowers begin to bloom, people begin to say hello. Everywhere you point forms take shape behind your fingertips, forms so remarkable you forget to know their names. And behind you the whole business is neatly rolled up and put away, so that it will all be as good as new the next time you come along.

Little girl, what's to become of the world, now that you're no longer here? Nothing will wake up any more, because it's not you who's coming along. The things have gone back to nodding drowsily the way they always did, sticking to themselves; we edge around them carefully so as not to disturb.

But still, I know right where you are. I can still feel you, your warm head resting in the palm of my hand, your little body atremble on my lower arm, your tiny fist clamped around my pinkie. Babydoll, I can still find my way right to you. Like that! I race up the stairs, tiptoe down the last stretch of hallway in stocking feet, in order not to rudely awaken you and your mama.

But when I stick my head around the corner, nothing's the way it should be any more. Every time I enter the bedroom, it's the wrong one. It seems that last time I pulled a door shut thoughtlessly behind me, and now, lost amid identical doors, I can no longer find the right one. *Because I only recognize it from the inside.* All the rooms I enter have become different rooms, even though they look strikingly like our own. But, looking back on it, the light is different. Duller, greyer. An extra layer on top of everything. Our house has become the house of other people, and we've become strangers in our own lives as well.

Happiness is so near, I can, as it were, reach out and grab it. When I lean over to touch it, I bump my head against thick glass; it's that near.

Everything is still here. The baby clothes, the playpen, the cot. Just in case. Just in case it all turns out to have been a big misunderstanding.

One must always be ready to welcome the dead, that's a known fact. For a long time, for example, my father continued to pay absolutely no attention to his own death. After his funeral, he just kept coming home. He had a place set for him at the table, he received his mail at the old address. He had parked the car (as the only one in the family who could drive) in its regular place. His raincoat hung on the hook by the door, his hat lay on the rack. His footsteps were heard regularly on the stairs, on the parquet, on the gravel in front of the house, he shut doors – upstairs, outside – behind him all the time. And when you got up to see what was taking him so long, you could still smell his tobacco in the hall: as if he'd just gone out the door and would come back in a bit. Sometimes I had to pull out the obituary just to convince myself that he was dead.

Since then other people have moved into our old home, so there's no one waiting for him there any more. We all moved to new houses, started new lives, leaving my father behind in the former, the dated, the past. Suddenly, one day the table stopped being set for him, his mail stopped arriving, his hats and coats disappeared from the rack, his footsteps were no longer heard and everyone stopped getting up to see what was taking him so long. Apparently he was dead then, without anyone being able to say exactly when it happened.

Time reconciles, they say. But that should be: time reviews. It's a review exercise. You keep on hashing things over and over, until you forget what it was like at first.

That's why Orpheus wasn't allowed to look back. By seeing her anew, he reviewed her. And so obliterated her.

You've withdrawn from the world and put yourself back in our hands. What you left behind are days to come that come to no one, an unmanned life that will always be there without a trace. A sudden appearance into thin air. The world has started to consist of places where you are not, time of moments without you. '*Nirgends, Geliebte, wird Welt sein als innen.*'* Rilke foresaw in the seventh of his *Duineser Elegien*, in lofty seclusion and with death at every window. Our world has become an inner world. We use it to save things that have no right to exist outside any more. More and more of what we look for can only be retrieved from our thoughts, no longer from the world around us.

You've become a figment. But is it really you? In every room the stillness screams that you're still there, the emptiness hides you at every clearing. 'And where you are is where you are not,' T. S. Eliot says somewhere, somewhere I can no longer find. The old mystical paradox. You are nowhere, because you're everywhere. But is it really you? Or have we simply given your name to the omnipresent lack?

The life of a child is the invention of the parents. They not only beget their child, but conceive it as well.

* 'The world, my beloved, will be nowhere other than within.'

I myself was conceived in a narrow age when people were afraid things could only get worse. My entire youth was spent disentangling myself from my parents' thoughts. Making sure I did not become the platitude they had come up with.

Later you realize that your other lives, the ones you've supposedly 'chosen yourself', are a figment as well. But of whose imagination? How many dirty old men have hitched a ride with me unnoticed? One lives in a pornographic universe, a place where others have already planned out what you consider to be your life. You never arrive anywhere as the first and only. It's all been done, seen, experienced. You're only there to do it again, to do it all over again. You forgot long ago what it means to be the first and only, because when you're the first and only anywhere, in a restaurant for example, it gives you the creeps. And what about in love? Awareness of another's envy makes dying passion flare up like a hot coal. No woman wants to walk beside a man others don't even look at. No man fails to enjoy seeing his wife as a strange woman; in other words, as a woman he'd like to snatch away from someone else in order to possess her. It's those damned other people, every time. And should you ever be alone, you hope it will be in the prescribed, prefabricated way: the way the singer tells us about it in his lyrics, the way the movie star plays it on the silver screen. No, even your so-called loneliness is an imitation.

Individuality is a model, a concept, a design. It's something you can point to when asked. That's why you want different lives, for if there's one thing you don't want to be, it's yourself. You want to keep changing all the time. That is: make a different person of yourself. Become someone else, so you yourself need not exist.

You, my sweet, were the best different person I could have hoped for. I no longer had to invent myself; I had you. The most fabulous lives lay before you. I had laid them out for you there myself, hoping they would fit you later on. I was your father, I could do no other, I had to imagine you. I still am imagining you, I can do no other, I can't just suddenly *not* think of you, can I? I think of you: I think you up. *Cogito ergo es*. You stayed too young to ever be able to walk away from me and invent yourself. You'll never be another, you'll never be able to free yourself from my thoughts. I can count on you here forever, here in the wings of our family theatre. While the curtains go up onstage and the audience in the darkened hall holds its breath, you are ready to go on. You are ready to go on for all time. Even when the crowd has gone home and the lights are out, you're still ready to go on.

How many times have I started all over again? The
discovery of a fundamental flaw, after which the entire
design needs re-engineering. Each time it turns out
that the life I've developed was based on obsolete
premises, faith (in my own ability, in a happy ending,
et cetera) has to be found again and again. And where
do I find it? Where have I, where have the ones I've
been, found it till now?

In starting anew. Inventing life all over again. In
trying again and again to catch in a skein of meaning
the experiences that slip through my fingers. In tying
things together to make a net, until it becomes a whole.

All my other lives, so what did I do with them? Some
of them I have put away neatly, others have been torn
to pieces in a rage, yet others have been left lying
around somewhere, while most of them have been put
out with the trash in tidy packages during the big
springcleaning. (Sometimes I see someone else walking around with one of them, one of those discarded
lives.)

To be sure, I have been a man, a boy, a young man
who never wanted children, who considered the family
a prison and could not fathom how someone might
'share' their life (with two people, three, four, until
there was very little of it left over). It was the kind of

cynicism that races out ahead of the empirical look, a wild-eyed negativism that needs its denials in order to withstand the flood of choices. How was I to know what it was like to have a child? For the longest time I clung to my 'freedom', being the freedom to remain standing in the doorway under all conditions, and so preserve the impression that I can do whatever I like.

Such considerations have now become completely foreign to me. I once had my life in my own hands, but now it's got its hands on me. I spurned death, but now I'm at home in it. I know where I have to get to in time: I've already been there.

And now?

Yes, what now?

FUTURE

Still, I hang on to old plans for the future. Like the cigar box secured with rubber bands in which a stubborn farmer keeps his expired banknotes: they just happen to express better his idea of what it is to be rich than the new currency does.

SUMMER NIGHT

Till deep into the summer night grown chilly we sit here, the café long closed, the patio under the plane trees all tidied up. Except for our table. Our words keep us together. We know that outside us, in the dark, the universe is sombrely quiet. What are we doing here? Why didn't we disappear long ago? But still, here we are. And as long as we keep talking we don't hear how quiet it is. In what we tell each other the lights are still lit, the glasses still gleam, the waiters still hurry back and forth.

Without our words we would flutter away into the night, dissolve into the cosmos. But as long as we can keep thinking ourselves up, here on this lost patio, on this sandbank in the sea of used-up time, as long as we keep thinking that we hear the moths pattering against the lamp outside, the glassware behind the bar inside still tinkling busily, still see the last pair of lovers exchanging kiss-shaped confidences at the little table in the corner, as long as our words can still meet each other's senses, we are sitting here quite comfortably, thank you.

In our thoughts there's still time to spare. We've kept sweeping most of it out in front of us, we've barely touched it at all, saved most to serve as buffer between us and the end. As far as we're concerned, we've just started.

Somehow, someway, we're not experiencing this evening, we're just sitting here longing for it. Longing for something that we're already losing. More and more silence keeps slipping through between our words. Silence, darkness, emptiness. And there you have it, just what we were afraid of: the moment slips from our hands and breaks into a thousand pieces.

We get up and walk off into space.

A child isn't so much born; rather, it appears to you. It is, quite literally, disclosed to you. Only then, only when someone else had taken me over from myself, did I see the world I'd wandered around in like a blind man for so long. Suddenly I knew what I was doing here, I was here to keep alive something tiny and beautiful, and I felt a helpless craving for those carefree songs that are like windows opened for air on a sunny morning.

During those first few days I was in desperate need of a soundtrack for my untuned euphoria; I felt like an actor in a movie old as a lifetime. In Paris, in New York, in all those dreamed-up movie-theatre towns, happiness always manifests itself at last right out there on the street: the crowd unfolds like a flower, everyone submits willingly to a role as extra in order to give the lucky devil all the room he needs.

It happened to me in real life while out shopping. I saw it in the plate-glass window of Hunkemöller Underwear, on which my leading role was being projected as I walked by. People had always got in my way, and now they were stepping aside. I couldn't believe my good fortune. Everyone laughed and applauded, everyone was happy for me. They were all shadows, I was the only one who really existed.

At the Free Record Shop, where the girls behind the counter chew their gum till all the feeling has gone out of it, I put down my bags full of family groceries and flipped through the racks of CDs in search of music for the film I'd ended up in.

I may not have known what I was looking for, but I knew exactly what I wanted: it had to be music that came about while it was being played, no 'perfect performance' or 'brilliant rendition'. Music that had to get used to itself, that had to get to know itself. Listening, I wanted to come into being as well, rather than be there to check whether it was all correct.

With a certain disdain, the gum-chewing girls behind the counter put on the CDs I'd culled from the various racks. I had trouble really listening at first; the headphone reeked of someone else's ears. Still, there was no getting around the fact that, at track 2 of *Charlie Parker with Strings*, 'Everything Happens to Me', the whole world began beaming, thanks to the diamond disguised as a tear in my eye. Parker had thrown open all the windows in the house and blew out all the evil spirits, one by one. The string section of the seasoned show band tried to smooth it all out, but the man on the alto sax showed no mercy; he whipped them all over the ballroom. And through the open windows breathed New York, where it had all really happened. I stood there, my grocery bags between my feet, and had to grab hold of the counter. I was sure I'd heard this number before; the purest memory is that of the past one has never known.

I had finally begun at the beginning, I heard Parker saying. *You saw your child being born, man, you can't get any closer than that.* And indeed, it seemed as though I had just been born myself. But it was more than myself; it was my child. Everything I'd known had been wiped out, I didn't recognize a thing. Everything started to exist all over again. At last I had the world in my hands.

If anything is still there, then it keeps to the shadows, to where the light (and so the eye) can't reach.

No heaven, but earth. No little angel, but a shadow child. A lily among the flowers.

The phone rings, the phone keeps ringing all the time. We don't answer it. There's no one who can tell us what we want to hear. For the moment we have no words to defend ourselves with, we're still not quite sure who we're going to be.

They keep asking how we feel, but we have nothing to show them. The only words we find are ones we don't want to say. They taste of other people's mouths. The more talk, the higher the pile of misunderstandings. We can't get over it, we're bogged down in it, suffocated by all the wrong words.

We hush ourselves a hole in the wall of words, one we can breathe through.

AND THE CROWD PARTS

The fire that destroyed her deserted body keeps burning inside me. My eyes scorch with it. I imagine myself immortal; I just died, yet still I'm standing here. Now that the dearest thing of all has been taken away from me, I've become invulnerable. All feeling has been yanked from my fists.

It's easier to hate people than to have to live with them. If it's true that sometimes the wrong people die, logic says that other people should be dead. A great many, if not most, of the living have become unbearable to us. Killing time in front of us, wasting life before our eyes. But waste away themselves? Oh no, not that. All these swaggerers, living as though they have all the answers. To have to see them, hear them, smell them.

We see ourselves on an island in a sea of people who threaten us. Who try to infect us with their indifference, their crassness, and all the rest of their smug-born dismissal of all differences, their encroachment on everyone not like them. The rabble attacked and defeated us while we were skinless, defenceless, helpless as a baby. They belittled us by being there big as life, even though we'd never asked them to. But now we don't care any more. Now nothing can ever be set aright anyway.

Today sorrow walks the streets in arms. When I approach, the crowd parts like a frightened flock, for here is no respecter of persons.

To get away from something, or to find something again, we climbed into the car and drove south for days. Our route wasn't marked anywhere; we drove on till the roads first became unpaved, then finally ended.

Here, beyond human habitation, was where we stayed. We hid ourselves away in a dark wood in the hills. It seemed familiar to me from some other time. Only it hadn't grown older. Because I myself had changed, however, there were many things I no longer recognized. How do you remember the woods? Definitely not by the individual trees. More by the cracking of branches beneath your feet, the smell of humus, the flurry of lizards on the stony path uphill.

Our shelter was a makeshift hunter's lodge, hung with the odour of wood smoke and slaughtered game.

At first, here in this seclusion, I was pounced upon by the fear of people, of psychotic killers who would rape you and then rip us open with serrated knives, who would carve their anonymous, misspelled hate into our bodies. Ears cocked, eyes wide open, I lay between the sheets at night and listened to the rustling, the panting, with which the darkness stirred.

Wild animals. I hoped.

Every morning at first light (while you were still asleep, dreaming of the three of us, as if that time was yet to come) I crept out of the house into the beginning blue. The light of the new day had to come from far below, and still to reach over the hilltops. It threw a cold-steel gleam on everything, as though I was seeing the leaves, the sky, reflected in calm puddles.

Squatting down amid the fallen leaves, I studied the tracks. Wild boar, a fox. I knew that, because I'd known them from childhood. In fact, my father knew them too. He had shown them to me back then.

As long as I went on my way, the forest rustled continually. Whenever I stopped to see what I had heard, the animals stood breathless as well. Until they forgot about me, and were there again. I peered through the underbrush, but my eyes couldn't penetrate the thick green of twigs.

Gradually the wood began opening up to me. I ventured my way in step by step. I wasn't heading somewhere, I was coming back to somewhere.

The strangeness fell shut behind me, like branches that swing back and wipe out the trail.

I walked and walked; my feet had almost forgotten about me. En route from the unspeakable to the speechless. I arrived in the world from before the loss, when everything was still on the point of happening. I lived through my return to the woods from which I had been absent for so long. Something was recovered, a way was found. A way out. That is to say: out of myself, because the self is the barrier people use to block themselves off from the great whole.

Regained familiarity with a life not personal: trees, beetles, adders, mushrooms. A lukewarm toad in the palm of your hand, bark you scratch off a pine branch like a scab. The perfume of needles, mosses, lichens. Soil, stone, sand. Feet, fingers. I touched the forest as though touching myself. The tips of my fingers had become the fingertips of the forest, with which it explored its own surface.

Waiting for me not much later, at an open spot, was a stag. It stood stiller than the trees around it, its antlers the only branches not moving in the morning's breath. In order not to break the spell, I tried to look like a tree as well. We stood there like that for a boundless moment. The stag looked at me with dewy eyes, and I looked back. Trust me, my eyes said: my hands, my feet, all this belongs to the forest.

But the stag didn't believe me. Though I myself believed unconditionally in the astounding animal, it broke the spell with a frightened start and leaped away from being there, unfollowable, leaving me behind.

I wanted to shout something but didn't know what, my words fell short.

There was nothing left but to go on, deeper into the woods.

I had to learn to speak again, and I could just as well start with the animals.

The days fall across her like centuries, bury her, no longer decipherable beneath the sand of antique empires, dead languages. We walk through her posthumous life as through an Etruscan dig, where some relics have been marked with chalk, the rest of the stones, the sand, swept aside. Probing for remnants of a greater whole that no longer exists, that never did exist, in a landscape that is fast asleep.

So much has remained unhappened, so much has never been. How would her Etruscan have sounded? How her voice? Where are the snows that never fell? A palace or some other folly could be rebuilt if necessary, but who can restore the kiss of a girl who never kissed? Who can unearth her scent, her smile? Every attempt at reconstruction leads to what never existed. The more desperately we try to know her, the more foreign she becomes.

Every road back is a road that leads us further, to places that are new to us. Behind us everything has been dissolved. Collapsed, destroyed, disappeared. At our heels begins the abyss. We've arrived in a world that was never hers, and that never will be ours. Every shard, every trace we try to interpret takes us further away from her.

Breaks she who was whole into smaller and smaller pieces.

If we don't watch out, she will never have existed at all.

When the two of us had been left behind amid all the living, who were stranger to us than one of the dead, I started drinking the mother's milk you saved. That was all we could do. Your body wasn't interested, it had no intention of stopping, it still held enough life for both of you. I drank the sacral fluid in little sips, while you saw to her empty little body.

You remained a mother right down to your finger-tips. With knowing hands you cared for what was left in the dented hospital cot: a doll that had to be washed and dressed and combed, because we were playing that it was alive. The skin so real, the little body even a bit warm: impossible to imagine that a thing so perfect didn't work. You double-checked everything, one by one: you counted her fingers (with their little nails), her toes (idem), felt her earlobes, her little nose, everything had to be touched to make sure. The body that had been known through and through now had to be learned by heart.

You bathed her, changed her nappy, gently brushed her curls. (So beautiful, I saw you thinking, hard to believe this child was made by people.) You brought her in readiness, because she was going away without us now, travelling alone for the first time, yes, they'd be coming for her any moment. You bathed her, rubbed her skin with ointment, gave her clean clothes, until it was finished and there was nothing left for you to do.

And suddenly your arms were so empty, you picked up the little body and clasped it to yourself, and rocked yourself that way till you were calm.

Sitting beside the cold, unwrinkled bed, I at last learned the taste of mother's milk. Almonds, I noted, and also something sheepish. I swallowed it with a certain caution, as though it were medicine and all I could do was hope I had the right illness.

Do you want it, the baby, the body, the baby's body? Do you want to hold it for a minute, you asked. It's so heavy, so heavy to hold. But no, you didn't say that. You asked me: do want to hold our baby? Our little girl, you said. Do you want to hold our little girl? You still can, the visitors will be coming, we're still together now.

The name Isa Thomése remains open for all time. Followed not by a full stop, but by a question mark. Elisa Makira Thomése. A package left unclaimed, a letter undelivered, a bill whose last reminder has expired.

I think back to that uncertain trying, that 'coming up' with names. Nothing was right, nothing was good enough. Every possibility seemed ridiculous. Sometimes we were even afraid to say it out loud, we scribbled our ideas on the backs of torn envelopes. Nah, not that. She hadn't even come yet, how could we know her name?

From my dog-eared years of childhood reading I remembered peoples whose royal children had to conquer their anonymity by brave ordeal, and so earn their own name.

Her name, that told me, would come later. What we were to call her in the meantime was dictated to us in our sleep by an angel with a thousand tongues. Commandingly, with no explanation. I wrote it down and passed it along to the powers that be. When her time came, she would have to live up to it herself.

But now that 'later' has arrived and her time will never come, and there is still that provisional, unplaced name.

It is the vacant chair at our table. It is the hook in the primary-school cloakroom where no coat ever hangs. It is the birthday party that can't be held. It is the neighbourhood playground where the children gather and no one's missing. The zoo where all the animals stand waiting, the man selling ice-cream in the park. The park where the light falls through the leaves, the light no one's walking in now. It's the red shoes in the shop window, you say; it's the bicycle another child is riding, I say. It's the family snapshots from the beach, the garden, the Christmas dinner, et cetera, with 'the whole clan' written on the back.

There is so much, and so much more (how much more, I'm not sure yet: the missing has only started) and through it all, her whole unlived life long, it must remain up in the air. She's dead, yes, but do things have to keep reminding us of that?

PANIC

The smell of clean sheets, the bedroom window open.
A new day.

    The sunlight coming in and finding her nowhere.

Sometimes I forget that the future is new. Then there's still the old one, that I can't get out of my head. I accidentally think it's all still waiting to happen. That's because there are just the two of us again. Like old times. Me the boy, you the girl, and what are we going to do, shall we go to the cinema, or we could hop in the car and drive to Brussels, I mean to Paris, we have plenty of time and no one's expecting us. We've grown years younger at a single blow, we've been tossed back into an old memory. We're expecting – what else? – great things. We uncork exotic wines deep into the night, and the clocks don't chime for us. We don't worry about an hour here or a day there, we can see to that ourselves.

You remember now, that we wanted a child later on? I still do, I say to you, and you still do too. And we act as though we haven't sneaked a look, we pretend not to know what our child will look like, or what its name will be. We act as though we don't know a thing, Isa.

So much future has become part of the past, so many possibilities have remained unused. Entire unlived lives have been dumped – sight unseen – from the future straight into the past. So that the possibilities are still lying there, as it were, waiting to be acted on in real life.

What does it matter, what you call a thing that's on its way but always stays beyond reach? You look ahead and your life takes shape behind your back. You point, but by then it's already behind you. It's been before it arrives. Things only really start once it's over. Later, you say, when everything was going to be all right. But was it later, or was it before, when everything was going to be all right? The further you go cartwheeling off into time, the harder it is to tell the two apart. You long for something, and have no idea whether it's already been or whether it still has to come.

'*Aus dem vergessen lockst du träume . . .*'* (Stefan George, 'Juli-Schwermut').

That's right, dreaming of what has been, you can do that too. How it was, and how it almost was. How it could have been, how it should have been, what it should be like. And, when you close your eyes: how it will be.

* 'From what is forgotten you conjure up dreams . . .'

When you've lost enough, the past finally becomes what the future used to be: a distance to dream away in, a horizon behind which there's always a second chance, and where, despite the pastness of it all, inexplicable hope lives on.

One sees best through the eyes of another. 'Look,' my father would say, and if I looked carefully I could see it too. We were outside, and what he pointed to in the bushes became birds. And the birds became different: chiffchaff, grosbeak, flycatcher. With my father's eyes I saw them, each and every one.

Until he died. Suddenly they were gone, the trees were still, everything had lost its tongue.

Right after my father was gone, when he was, as it were, almost still alive, I had the feeling I had to act as his observer, in case his death proved a passing thing and he would have to be brought up to date afterwards.

Those were days of an extreme keenness, because I was looking for two. It was as though I had to keep the world from falling apart, on my father's behalf. If I didn't look carefully, the whole thing would simply collapse. So many things had a right to exist only because of his look, and without that look would be lost. It was up to me to look the way he would have, to see what he would have seen. And it struck me: a dead person sees more than you might imagine. He knows exactly what's no longer there, he knows every road fallen into disuse.

But once, when I wasn't paying attention, I lost him.

The way you look at the cracks in a wall or a ceiling and suddenly can no longer see the lines that made a shape, that's the way I lost my father's look one day, and my eyes couldn't find him back again.

The world of the living is a world where too little attention is paid. The dead obviously have little to say about the matter. No one sees what they saw any more. There are too few observers, they're too busy living themselves, everyone is, to look for someone else, to look for two.

Unless, perhaps, it's the occasional starry-eyed lover: he looks around shyly through the eyes of a person he doesn't know yet, everything around him he sees only now for the first time, only now for real. Even she who, time after time, is more than he can remember. He looks, looks and looks again, but she's barely turned the corner and everything's a riddle once more.

I'm reminded of these, of the lovers' look and the eyes of the dead, because this is about your birth now, Isa, and I went out to tell the world about it. Because the world might not have noticed, might not have known that it had changed for good.

On the bike to the registrar's office I saw nothing and everything at the same time. In the crystal-clear morning streets that spilled over me the world became more beautiful than it could ever have been of its own accord.

I found things waiting for someone I'd forgotten to

miss for so incredibly long, but whom I had to look for now as though my life depended on it. My eyes had to save it all, I couldn't forget a thing. I looked for two, because later on I'd have to tell it all to my sweetest little girl.

If the idea of a deity comes from anywhere, it must be from the dead. Unreachable, untouchable, but still so terrifyingly familiar. (In Hölderlin's words: 'Nah ist/ Und schwer zu fassen der Gott.'*)

I'd never thought of that before, or at least I'd never thought my way through the words. But then again, never before had dying been so close. So close it feels as though it has happened in me, my insides full of dead spots.

A deity, like a dead person, is a wanderer with no body left. A drifter now dependent on the thoughts of others. But people don't really know how to think of either a dead person or a deity. They're too careless. They think too grandly about deity, and inflate it to mega-sized capitals: Creator, Allah, Yahweh, Lord of Lords. Ridiculous bombast. A deity is something slight and frail. Recognized by almost no one. Maybe because it's too close.

It's hard to think of someone without a body. So when it comes to the dead, you keep the former body in mind, just to be sure. But at the same time you know that, in any case, you'll never see her again *that* way. That's a fact of chemistry. And so you begin toying with thoughts of a deity; their form – as we all know – is not subject to rules hard-and-fast.

* 'So near/Yet hard to grasp is God.'

You can't think her into being whenever it suits you; a deity waits for suitable thoughts. As I have noticed. The force of will, in this case, amounts to nothing. A deity appears inside you when *she* feels like it.

Because they have no body left but still remain present, after their fashion, they create the impression of being immortal. Which is not the case, of course; the only thing that is immortal is the thing that's never lived.

A deity draws her power from having become nothing but thought. Wherever she is, she's never alone. That's what it comes down to. There is always someone around her, keeping her in his thoughts. Addressing the deity therefore means: talking to yourself. With a voice unfamiliar to you as your own. Usually not understandable, but that's not the point: nothing is being conveyed. It's language staying in.

And all that time she'd been hidden in the future, waiting for me. All that time stopped dead, for me to come along. That's how things had been arranged, only no one had told me.

The premise is a classic one, performed on countless occasions. The father powerless to save his child. The gods know it, the audience has already seen it in the libretto. Only Dad is completely ignorant. Spurring on his hobbyhorse through wind and rain.

I must have read such stories often enough, heard about them, watched them, but then I wasn't the father. Then I was someone else. (Someone who embraced the extreme without ever learning that the outmost boundary knows no way back. Who – dreaming of extremes from the safety of his golden mean – thought reality was worthless in the hands of normal people, that reality needed the style of extremist writers to become charged with meaning. That going to extremes was a matter of style.)

Now that I've arrived here, at this spot reserved for me in the universe, I no longer understand my mentors. I've been cut off from them, their words no longer draw me in. They remain suspended on the hallowed shelf.

Like a stranger I leaf through favourites such as

Laughter in the Dark and *L'Éducation sentimentale*. There was something in both of them about children dying, wasn't there? But what was it? Apparently something that could be forgotten.

When I find the passages I was looking for, I realize why I'd forgotten them. They are passages: in both Nabokov and Flaubert, the main character loses – *en passant*, in the space of a paragraph or two – a child, and then the story picks up where it left off. But don't they have to learn to walk, talk, live all over again? Flaubert at least dedicates a fine phrase to the inconsolable mother: '. . . and her sorrow increased her mother-hood.' But by then Frédéric Moreau already has his coat on, *en route* for the desirable Mme Arnoux, and he will never again, not once in the next hundred pages, think back on his lonely, ice-cold, stone-dead child.

Not even the *Erlkönig*, that classic of child mortality, can – at this hour of the night – find a willing ear with me. We met once, either before or after coffee during intermission at the Concertgebouw, partway through the evening's song recital full of Teutonic gloom. But, back then, what did I know? Even Goethe himself had no idea: like Mahler composing the *Kindertotenlieder* unawares, the Olympian too put his luckless father to rhyme before setting eyes on his own fate.

And like everyone else I'd been enthralled by how Schubert made Death's breakneck pursuit (the gallop with which the horseman tries to escape with his sick child is the same gallop with which Death stays on their heels) 'take part' in the piano accompaniment: the wind in the alders, the sparks flying from the hooves, you can hear it in the left hand, the right hand.

But now that I should 'really' understand it, I no longer understand. The same way I no longer understand Nabokov and Flaubert. Their words are other people's words about other people, the kind one says about something or someone, precluding, conclusive words.

And indeed, for others this little life is shut like a box with her name on the lid. For others, yes, it's one of those things that happens to others. Something you can sum up in sweeping terms, the way every day and all over the world horrors are summed up in such or so many words.

But for me, the word well chosen, the word that struts its own brilliance, is a thrust to the heart, Monsieur Flaubert, a devastation, Mr Nabokov. A bomb going off at the heart of what I'm trying to approach so carefully.

You don't leave a blank page anywhere, there's nowhere I can get through to my own blankest ignorance. You put full stops everywhere and pull doors shut behind you. (Yes, even you, Herr *Geheimrat* Goethe. Your poem should not have ended with '*In seinen Armen das Kind war tot*'.* That's how it should have started.)

* 'In his arms the child was dead.'

Everywhere, doors of consolation are being quietly closed behind me: cynical doors, touching doors, distant doors, familiar doors, complacent doors, how-could-I-forget doors, doors of denial, maudlin doors, careful doors, arrogant doors, worn-down doors.

No, I say, none of that. Don't close a thing. The doors need to be open. Let them be jemmied, kicked out of their frames. Let the wind blow through, let it be cold.

Livy tells us how it was the Romans' custom, in desperate times, to 'read' the entrails of sacrificial animals. The liver in particular could provide the initiated observer, the *haruspex*, with useful tips.

In the young, powerful world of those days, there was a great deal that could be predicted. There was so much future that everyone had their own way of looking at it.

It depended only on what you were willing to see. In the oak leaves of Dodona the riddles rustled like animals fleeing the hunt, the Sibylline books in fat volumes delivered oracles that went far beyond the transient world, and on her tripod at Delphi the Pythia gurgled parts of speech from the deepest depths of her thoughtlessness, there where we become an other ourself. On top of all that, moreover, came the bottomless reply of the ever-advancing night, where a thousand times thousands of shimmering stars winked their secrets to those wise enough to see them.

But also, and more than all the rest, the liver could provide those in a quandary with insight into the gods' will. Some claim that haruspication was handed down from the Etruscans; others trace its origins to the Chaldeans.

The sacrificial child we had brought from home was

carried by the *augurium* into the inner temple, where we couldn't go, and opened there with a razor-sharp scalpel. I had no idea what her liver, which had been unable to save her, could ever teach us. Purifier of the blood, but not her blood.

They read her like a book slammed shut at the final page. The story, it seemed, was a familiar one.

We were advised to rely on the stars from here on out.

The first one to see it was a farmer out ploughing his field near the Etruscan city of Tarquinii. His iron ploughshare struck something hard. A stone, he thought, but it was a child's head, sticking up out of the red earth.

A remarkably old head it was, with thin grey hair, waiting patient as a plant for the farmer's hand to pull it from the ground.

This was how it had to be. But the farmer didn't know that. He looked at the old child, incredibly young and unbelievably wise, and didn't know what to think. Not even when the harvested one announced that he was Tages, and claimed he could remember the future.

Afraid of what he did not know, and hoping never to find out, the farmer ran off over the hills, back to his people. He needed the consent of others in order to believe his own eyes. Only in the midst of many did he dare to return to the field where he had made his remarkable discovery.

But the old child was no longer there. Even the hole he had dug with his own hands was nowhere to be found. As though none of it had happened.

In his book about telling the future, however, Cicero claims that the old child actually did appear to the crowd of villagers: not from a hole in the ground, but from a cloud above the fields. A cloud of smoke being blown in their direction. From that temporal throne, the god-child, old in knowledge, spoke to the assembled Etruscans. He taught them to read their fate in certain signs, he predicted what lay in wait for them.

They, down there on the ground, did their best to remember their future. (But it was so strange to them, so implausible.)

What the Etruscans later thought they remembered was written down by augurs in the *Libri Tagetici*, known also as 'the books of fate'.

They contained what the old child had taught them: the way the future leaves its tracks in so-called 'signs'. For everything that was yet to come was already there. But also the things that were *not* to be, so spoke the child who was born old and entered young into death's realm, were all established beforehand.

At the end of the day we were called in. Even as a little boy I had known that meant no good. The office. Sitting there at the desk was an adult, grey and fleshy, placed over me only in order to punish me. He didn't like it any more than I did, he said then, punishing didn't solve anything, he knew that too, but he had no choice in the matter, there was nothing he could do about it.

Ever since it has remained a place where one ought not to be, a place where, in a certain sense, one actually isn't. You situate your body politely in a chair and take off right away in your thoughts, leaving the body to its fate with acquired nods and gestures, the activity of speaking switched over to the automatic talker.

There inside the place into which we had been called, everything had been carefully stripped of meaning. The spare props were all made of washable material. The people who manned it at set hours were, it seemed, not allowed to leave a trace. One just happened to be on duty there, just as on that day we happened to be the ones who had to be given the news.

Everywhere around the world are little offices where life and death are ruled over by people who have to be home by six. That hour had, by the way, almost arrived; many floors below, on the earth, the first worked-up commuter traffic was making its way homeward.

It never gets easier, I believe someone was saying from behind the desk, everyone here would rather bring good news, but sometimes it just doesn't work out that way.

I tried to figure out whose phrases these were, but there was no one speaking personally. Or did this man in the white coat simply go with the situation? That almost had to be the case. The disorder fell within his specialism, and its terminal phase within his hours on-duty; that's why (he said) he was the one who happened to be sitting across from us.

And what was going on inside you? You had left your body behind in the chair beside me, I saw, in a pose that hadn't changed for quite a while. You still had the yearning look of someone who has only just started waiting, and who can't believe there will be no more trains stopping at this station.

Was I actually here myself? Yes, those were my own hands I recognized, it turned out I had clasped them together like someone who has scooped up a ladybird and doesn't want to let it fly away.

The moment arrived when apparently everything had been clarified. I simply nodded my head yes, because then we'd be allowed to leave. We were already getting up. (To search outside for thoughts under quiet trees.) The man in the white coat routinely showed us to the door, then left himself. The cubicle was, as it were, folded up and put away. No one would have any more need for it today.

The day was done. The lucky ones all arrived home before dark.

Like a mollusc in its shell, I withdrew into my inner chamber. In the dead of night, staring at the first words to appear on my screen, waiting for their possible meanings.

Somewhere in the language she is still there, somewhere between a word or two. Words that don't know each other yet. And that don't know her yet.

Writing is trying out sentences to see what they might mean. Becoming a newcomer in the idiom, a beginner, and asking for the unknown. It's finding what can't be looked for, because it only started existing the moment it was found.

If she's still there, then it's in the words I wait for at night. Sometimes I still feel her too, but my arms, my hands, my skin are less, less and less, used to her.

Things are coming back to me one by one, it's true, but they're not the way they used to be. They remain replicas, perfect imitations of something that doesn't exist on its own. The apparent, copied right down to the slightest detail. No one seems to see the difference, but I see it at a glance.

Because the absence I feel is not something I can 'get over'. It's there all the time, wherever I go. Wherever I show up, things fall silent. Not the life and soul of the party, no. (Did someone forget to shut the window, or a door? No, no, it's only me.)

Otherwise I simply remain the other person I've always been. The one I'm forced to imitate wherever I go, don't worry about that. The man with my name, my address, my life. A person with a story, a meaning, who moves his lips to form a word, who uses his mouth to make words out of nothing.

There is no last moment, the moments always keep on going, there is no end to the dying. It only changes shape all the time.

First she dies in our arms, grows heavier than she'd ever been (because there's nothing left to bear her up, no winged soul to propel her tiny body up and up against the pull of the earth). That which has kept her going has now been transferred to us. Now we have to be sure to keep her. That makes us heavier. Or does it bear us up? Do we become lighter? Only dying will tell. (Dying: another word for time.)

And meanwhile she goes on dying all the time. In her little body, becoming colder and stiffer, but also at home (where no one's home at this particular moment): in her nursery, her clothes, her bottles and things, in her photos and her books, her stuffed animals, in her pram in the hallway.

And then she begins to die outside as well, even in places where she never was, in the minds of people she never saw. In minds that are turned away, in shame, from fear of being contaminated, out of cowardice. In minds where she is denied and quietly put to death.

But above all she dies in us. There where she has been thought of, there she must die. There where she will be thought of, there she will have to be dead. But it is impossible, and it will remain impossible, not to think of her. At last, therefore, there will be no place left where she has not died.

It's only just started. She has at least a lifetime to go.

'Death speaks in me,' Blanchot says. Every word speaks of an absence, every word expresses a lack. To know something is: to know something is lost. I say it, but it's already gone. Where language is, there insufficiency is gauged. Only when a thing is gone do you find the words for it. And so every word becomes an afterword, every sentence an epitaph.

Et cetera, et cetera.

But it is all I have. She is nowhere else but in language. Her molecules have passed irrevocably into new C-, H- and O-compounds, no laboratory can put them back together in their original configuration. Only in the still-unwritten alchemy of words can she keep trying to exist.

Lifted from her body and laid in words. She has become someone who must make certain she is born over and over: in the words I find for her.

They are words that do not apply everywhere, they can't have other people around. Like Jesus in the house of Jairus, when he used magic words to bring the man's daughter back to life. '*Thalita koumi*,' the Lord said, after ordering all windows and doors to be closed, for he hated people looking over his shoulder. ('Girl,' the magic words mean, 'I say to you: arise.') And the girl arose, seen by no one but her parents. 'Yet he bade them tell it to no one,' Mark writes.

Blanchot, in his philosophy of language, goes further than Jesus. I understand him to say that reality goes on dying, and that it is only the words that continue to rise again.

But what else can they say except mourn, if they do nothing but point to a world that has just died on the tip of one's tongue? What else can they be, but like Jairus's daughter, who can only come to life as long as that remains unshared?

Atop the city of the past a new city has arisen, one in which the one I miss has lived and moved. The new-born streets look at me strangely, some unaware; others – caught in the act – can barely suppress a giggle. Yet others, guilty and with eyes downcast, allow me to pass like a one-man funeral procession. 'This city,' they say, 'has been built only for you, so that you can wander here on your own, while the people remain in that other city, so as not to disturb you.'

Those I see are shades of the former life, apparitions I've forgotten to forget, who have remained tangled in the cobwebs of memory. I do not greet them as I pass, just as one does not greet photos or headstones.

I'm in the new city on my own, a survivor among phantoms.

The phantoms don't know that it has happened, they do all they can to look like living people and throng together in places where they are many. Their behaviour reminds me very much of the former city, when I too did my utmost to look like living people, mostly by drinking beer in cafés and talking, talking, talking. To someone or to no one, in principle that didn't matter much.

Now it's quiet, I can't make out what anyone is

saying. No meaning gets through to me, none of it says a thing to me. To live you must be afraid of death, you must have something to lose. There must be something left, something you *haven't* lost.

I have returned as a stranger to this ruined and resurrected Troy, to this city built on the dead. It's morning, but still dark when I arrive, everything cold and blue as still water. If I screamed it would all start to ripple; if I stopped everything would again be clear and dead. And if I didn't make a sound, it would be no different.

Again I was reminded of your birth, that eruption compared with which your death was no more than yet another change of shape, a breath of wind, a ripple on the water.

And I continue to keep it in mind, so I can tell you about it later on. How you appeared, floundering like a slippery little mammal, swimming from the erupting mother physical. A life was unleashed, a world created that was immediately your own.

Your mother and I looked at each other and saw each other as never before. We didn't know whether to laugh or to cry, so, just to be sure, we did both.

And you just lived; I had never met anyone as alive as you before. If anyone was little, there in the women's quarters, it was me. I made myself small, drew in my arms and feet so that your attendants would lose no valuable time. You called for hot-water bottles, warm towels. Clean sheets for your bleeding mother. You demanded all available life for yourself. Your umbilical cord had to be severed, for you had landed here on earth to find a place for yourself. You had come to stay. To be here for ever.

And again I find you, and again you're not the one. The recollection demands new words all the time, I'd forgotten that, they have to keep moving. Not freeze. No pictures, please. A memory needs enough room to keep being recollected. It must be able to hide in places where no one looks. In words where no one's expecting it.

A recollection can light up in our memory only once. Flash! Then it freezes into the photo of a falsified eternity. Because 'just like', that's never been. Not even 'back then'. Yarns to clutch at. In fact, a re-memberer always moves away from his dead, towards his own death. That movement is life. A thing lives only in the course of dying.

So don't try to hold on to anything, not even the loveliest, especially not the loveliest. Keep trying to let it go, keep acknowledging the gap as it grows. Always be willing to stand there empty-handed. That makes it easier to catch whatever's tossed your way.

A man returns, the story has often been told. He had sailed away across oceans of ignorance, to lands which ultimately lay beyond even those horizons. Troy, they called it there, City of the Annihilations, from which one comes back alive only in order to tell about it.

After years of hardship the man goes home, where he never arrives. The impossible return. No one, says Heraclitus, steps into the same river twice. No one comes back to what he has left behind.

Home: the invention of strangers. Dreamed up to lend direction to the straying, to let one think, while disappearing into no-man's-land, of a place where everything stays the same, where the best memories actually exist in real life.

Odysseus' hatred of those who remained behind, of the so-called 'suitors', when he returns to Ithaca and there, standing on the coast of yore, discovers that he will never come home again. The returnee's rage at the ignorance that has lived on in his absence, the total ignorance of those who stayed behind concerning what he went through after the destruction of god-loved Troy, during his impossible, almost lifelong 'homecoming'. Rage too at the self-deception that made him forget that his return

was a figment, and that he, Laertes' quick-witted
son, back at last upon the shores of Ithaca, would
miraculously have remained the same.

You hear it only bit by bit. First, on the white and the black keys, the hands perform their familiar play: on the left the deliberate fall and rise of the old bass chords, on the right, sparkling like sunlight on water, the young, high notes. But the high ones begin to fall and the low ones rise, the two melodies flow from one hand to the other. They dance nimbly across the full expanse of keys, after each other, away from each other. There's no telling which hand is doing what. And then it suddenly emerges from the notes: a new melody. Coming not from either of the hands alone, but from both. It soars above them, it sings counter to them. As though trying to flee from every note it meets. It leaps over them, dives under them. If the hands aren't careful, it's lost in a wink.

That is the third voice. There are pianists who have to sing along with their hands in order to hold on to it, because the first and second ones are there the whole time, too.

When I write, I look for that voice. The way notes that didn't know on paper that they belonged together seem to thread themselves along to form the tones of a third melody, so too I try to find sentences not written in so many words, that can be read into without knowing precisely where they're at.

One, two, three. There is form, there is content, and there is something else. And those three are not easily separated. The left hand the father, the right hand the mother, and in both hands, but also in neither one of them, the child. One, two, three. Something is being said, it's being said in a certain way, but it's about something else. The third one, the actual one. The real one. No hands of its own, no need to hold on to anything, no need to touch. Sometimes I sing along with that third, with that elusive soprano, in order not to lose her, but now that's no longer necessary, now I follow her through everything, over all.

But I have to write to hear her; on her own she's nowhere.

Timidly, we carry our sick child down the stairs. So that no one sees us, so that no one asks. Do we have everything? Car keys, nappies, tissues, an extra blanket? The slaughter of the innocents has come to Bethlehem, and we – relying on certain signs – are trying to get away.

It's a strange route of escape that takes us to Egypt, this Sunday morning in April. Hurrying first behind the wheel, you with the carrycot on the backseat, straight through the Sinai of South Amsterdam, to the emergency service of which the voice spoke. There the two of you are transferred to an ambulance. Walkers stop and stare. Peer with hard, violent eyes. We act as though we don't exist, because anyone spotted in these parts is in a bad way.

And deeper into the wilderness. To the hospital, we're told. The shrill light of the ambulance races off like the wind in the blue morning streets. I, the superfluous Joseph on his donkey, follow at an immediately unbridgeable distance.

Asking the way everywhere, along identical hospital corridors, for only I among the three of us is not led by the Spirit. The unknown angel on the phone had said: 'Arise, and take the young child and its mother, and flee into Egypt, and be thou there until I bring thee word.' But where is Egypt? No signs point to it anywhere.

Here they can't help us, we're told. Here we cannot stay.

They give us our child in a plexiglas carrycot, for all to see. Curious Islamites crowd around us right away, they've come here to gather stories for the coffeehouses. With their dark, reflective eyes they form words to carry with them on clouds of dust and camelback.

But it must not be. What they are trying to see must not be thought. Fearful and ashamed, I stand in their line of sight, bend protectively over our deathly ill little girl, cover her up with my own thin shadow. As long as no one knows, there's nothing to worry about. As long as fear can't latch on to facts, it doesn't have a chance with us.

Back to the ambulance, once again the shrill and flashing light. And me, an experienced donkey driver by now, following along on my own. Deeper into the wilderness once more, further down a road that takes shape only once it's behind us. *In deserto* they call that in Church Latin. *Desertum*: desert, wilderness, past participle of *deserere*: to abandon, to give up, to desert. The hagiographers use it for situations in which even God fails to show up.

Abandoned and deserted, we search for a way through the wilderness called Desolation, the two of you far ahead (but where? but where?) and me back here, in an alarming imitation of through traffic, gasping for breath on this quiet road at a stoplight that has suddenly turned red just for me.

The cups, the glasses on the counter, the crumbs on the plates, crusts, peels, pips, the sludge in the drain: not so long ago, people still lived here. The newspapers lying open, the books marked with letters, hairpins, pencils between page this and page that, the last dregs of wine in the bottle, the torn-open letters: everything points clearly to that. The crumpled bed, the tossed clothing, kicked-off shoes, a sock: it's as though, any moment –

The green standby light on the computer, the bike keys on the table, the drop hanging from the shower-head, the address book scratched full beside the phone, an overfull drawer that refuses to close, the toothpaste cap, a basket full of freshly dirty laundry: everything here seems as though –

The daylight that reaches far into the rooms with its white gold, that makes the polished wood gleam shyly. On the walls, living, breathing paintings that want to be seen. Dust that suddenly glistens in a spot of sunlight. In a vase, tall red roses in late bloom, they spill their first petals and pollen on the tabletop. A window that stands ajar, a curtain that puffs up and falls back: as though, any moment, the door –

Hey, there they are. New people? The same ones? Who can tell? One thing's for certain, though: they just go on living. Oh yeah. They wash the dishes, put them back in the cupboard, they fold up the papers, straighten up the books, they make the bed, toss clothes into the basket, throw washing into the machine, open the windows to air things out.

And for the rest they fold up the playpen (how does that go?), gather up the toy animals, the music boxes, the picture books, put away the baby clothes, the bedding in a lock-tight plastic box that protects them from musty cellars. The hot-water bottles, the nappy-changing mat. The vitamin drops, the thermometer. The piles of nappies. Everything into a cardboard box. It has to happen, so it happens. The bassinette. The cradle. The cot, for later. Whatever can be taken apart has to be taken apart, the nuts and bolts separately, in a plastic bag, that's handier. For safekeeping? For the time being, they put everything out on the landing. When you see it all together like that, it's quite a big move, they tell each other.

She comes from far away, she hails from long ago, she's from before there was language.

For someone like that, everything is different. They must learn how to grasp the familiar. Speechlessness reigns where she comes from; there was nothing there for her to clarify. Here, where knowledge makes so many things imperfect, it's not like that. Here everything has already been thought to pieces.

She seems so much older and wiser, from an age long before ours, when thoughts were a void like huge frozen lakes.

I look at our little child lying naked, clothed only in drips and electrodes, her eyes closed beneath the artificial sun of medical science.

Is she there? Or are we alone? (Sometimes we have a hard time seeing her apart from ourselves. Especially you, who carried her for so long, can't completely distinguish between her and yourself. An unprecedented, inexplicable part of us, a remnant from the ice ages, no longer able to be understood.)

'She's closer to death than we are,' I venture. After all, hadn't she just left the darkness behind? Except for that, of course, I have no idea either. *Can't I, God damn it please, can't I just go instead of her?*

But then, she can deal with the situation so much better than we can. She only lies there, while we cry and cry. Not her, she only does that when she has to.

'Sentimentality is a failure of feeling,' says Wallace Stevens in his *Adagia*.

Sentimentality shrinks and cheapens suffering into something a person can look down on. Death, not as an abyss, but as the great divide. Not a nothing, but a something. Not a disappearance without end, but a last gasp.

Despite the spectacular scenes it often makes, when it comes right down to it sentimentality keeps everything neatly within bounds. Its suffering is never untold. The suffering comes free of charge. See the parasites of sorrow at the untimely funerals of public figures. Once everyone has recovered from the initial shock, the curtains can be pulled aside and everyone goes home feeling relieved.

A person who weeps usually has himself under control. A feeling you can express is a feeling you can handle. It has taken shape, it can be recognized, named, classified. A person who weeps is out to influence his surroundings.

It's an exploration of where one stops and the other begins, a flowing-over from yourself to another.

When I weep, someone else weeps inside me. I perceive him as someone who is trying to make something happen without me, as someone who has a more sharply defined view of me than I do, and who boldly claims to represent my true self.

Sentimentality is self-pity. It's suffering for its own sake, without having to actually undergo that suffering. On the sentimental tack, after all, you see yourself as 'someone', as someone else. Someone in whom you recognize yourself, as with a movie star; as someone, in other words, worth watching.

As soon as you surrender to sentimentality, you become another. You leave the dream state within the 'I' (which is like the breathing wind over the face of the earth) and start to be someone. Someone who bears a striking resemblance to someone else. Or simply someone you might meet on the street. You take on contour. 'No one' becomes 'someone'. 'I' becomes a character. The endless becomes bound.

Your 'I' is put into a box, and you carry that box around under your arm. Occasionally you lift the lid to show what's inside. 'That's me,' you say. 'I can even cry if necessary.'

There is a feeling, too, that holds its breath, that goes white as a sheet, because chasms are yawning all around. The best thing it can do, therefore, is abandon itself and turn to stone.

Everything freezes, that's how cold and quiet it grows. So cold that all feeling leaves you. So quiet that your breath freezes to your lips like a question mark.

Nothing happens any more, 'the next moment' has been frozen for all time. Like Siberian hunters in polar ice, like mammoths in the primeval world. So close, so unapproachably close.

And then the moment came that we would have to see her die.

Their duty almost finished, the sleepless night shift came to life. Around her bed the eavesdropper's curtain fell: the tragic one-acter could begin.

I felt myself becoming another, someone I'd never been before.

Behind the curtain zoomed and beeped the comatose monotony of the remaining cots. Deathless machines pumping blood and oxygen through little bodies out of order.

Morning had come, yet up here it remained night. We still existed, it seemed we hadn't died yet. Groping blindly for each other's sleeve or anything, part of a hand or wrist, a finger.

Then came the explanation of how easily it all went, but I couldn't keep my thoughts together, my thoughts couldn't keep me together, we drifted further and further apart.

It could only take place once I was no longer there. The drips, electrodes and tubes were removed, the monitors jumped to zero. A sigh, you said. I couldn't tell for sure. Close as it was, the moment itself seemed to escape me, as though she was keeping it for herself, our little girl, taking it with her quietly into her own absence.

Each time I think back on it, I realize I wasn't paying attention. The futility of it. A candle being blown out, and nothing more. Somewhere a door blows open and . . . fft.

It came as a shock, how heavily her body lay in our arms. That was it: such heaviness. Berry-blue spots arose on her cheeks, they didn't belong there. And she just kept sleeping, her temples white as chalk.

Language has no intention of understanding me, of giving me its parole. The words, deathless still, tumble through the air like swallows. They won't let themselves be lured by the stale bread of meaning, they won't be nailed like bats to my stable door. They dazzle high above the commonplaces, where the air is rarer than breath, the world whiter than paper.

TRANSITION

The changing of seasons, the fading of day into night. You sit in a field somewhere and you look and look, but you don't see where it ends. At a certain point the darkness seems to have taken over; all that's left of things are the shades, the black silhouette.

You sit in the chair beside the hospital bed and hold your child in your arms. It lives and it lives, but little by little it is dead.

To see a limit, you must see both sides of the limit. The one and the other. But here there is no transition. No moment when. No 'just now it was . . .'

Looking back, there is nothing of a 'till now' anywhere in sight. The seconds tumble over cliffs, in no time there yawns the chasm of for ever and always. Having arrived here, on this chair beside this empty bed, there is suddenly nothing else any more, nothing else but nothing.

This is how you bear it: you're not around. It happened out there, I didn't know what to do, I was standing at the window and I couldn't do anything, I couldn't lift a finger, I couldn't open my mouth, I couldn't get there, I couldn't move my legs. Apart from her I was. (It's as though, when it comes right down to it, the experience is suspended. You hold your breath, and only breathe out again once it's over. While it's happening, no one exists for a moment.)

Reality as something outside us, while we sit inside, imprisoned in ourselves: this is the dilemma which the American transcendentalist Emerson brings into focus in his essay 'Experience', when he claims that the death of his little Waldo did not really touch him.

'We animate what we can, and we only see what we animate.' Never can the subject loose its own bonds and break through to the other side.

Even the death of his child can't free him of himself. Or should I say: the death of his child in particular?

In total blindness, that's how you undergo what happens. You don't see that which is new, that which is unknown. How could you? You know nothing but comparisons, see nothing that doesn't resemble something else. In your mind you leaf quickly through the Big Picture Book of Homemade Knowledge. You latch on to that which looks familiar: doorknob, sink, electrical cord, fluorescent lamp, but what escapes you is the link between these things, the unique connection that constitutes the once-only essence of this situation. Plexiglas bedstead, monitor, needle. The situation keeps falling apart into props and labels.

'I cannot get it nearer to me,' Emerson says of the impossibility of obliterating the dividing line between subject and object. 'So it is with this calamity; it does not touch me.'

I would say exactly the reverse. Not that it doesn't touch me, but that I don't touch a thing. The situation doesn't need me, it's constantly held back from being there, as it were, by my obtrusive presence. I am the one who – with his endless attempts to comprehend – makes this situation incomprehensible.

Without me everything could be itself, would be freed from the tiresome need to transpose itself into a language in which it can't express itself properly.

If I would only leave the room, it could finally come crashing down in peace.

A NOTE ON THE AUTHOR

Pieter Frans Thomése won the AKO Literature Prize for his debut *Zuidland* (*Southland*) in 1991. *Shadow Child* is his sixth book, and has been translated into fourteen languages. He lives in Haarlem, the Netherlands, with his wife Makira and his son Frederik.

A NOTE ON THE TYPE

The text of this book is set in Bodoni Book. Giambat-
tista Bodoni designed his typefaces at the end of
the eighteenth century. The Bodoni types were the
culmination of nearly three hundred years of evolution
in roman type design. Bodoni is recognized by its high
contrast between thick and thin strokes, pure vertical
stress, and hairline serifs.